Mirrored Reflections

Kakul Hai

BookLeaf Publishing

India | USA | UK

Presentation by *BookLeaf Publishing*

Web: www.bookleafpub.com

E-mail: info@bookleafpub.com

ISBN: 9789360942526

First edition 2024

DEDICATION

To my family
Seemin Hai, Abdul Hai, Sameera Hai Baig, Arif
Baig, Noreen and Adnan

ACKNOWLEDGEMENT

It is impossible to produce anything creative without inspiration. I am extremely lucky to come from a family of people who have been both intellectually and creatively blessed, and who have inspired me throughout the course of my life. If I can live up to the standards set by them, I would consider my life to have been meaningful.

More than inspiration, support is essential. My parents, Seemin and Abdul Hai, and my sister, Sameera, have provided me with unimaginable support in whatever I have chosen to do in my life. They have also been the biggest fans of my writings. The happiness that they feel whenever I write anything is heartwarming. More than me, they have been most excited about the publishing of this book!

My brother-in-law, Arif Baig, has always had more faith in my writing talent than perhaps even me. Immensely talented himself, his photograph adorns the cover of this book. I thank him for allowing me to use one of his creations for my first book.

Noreen and Adnan, my niece and nephew, I hope I can inspire you to go achieve your fullest potential like the rest of my family members have inspired me to do. If I can play even a small part in their life journey, I will feel extremely fulfilled.

A shoutout to my cousins, Huma, Nikhat and Ayhan, all writers themselves… you are my inspiration, in life in general. Thank you for being you and giving me the place in your life that you have.

And of course, my biggest support system in the past few years, Utkarsh, who every day insisted that I write, write, and write! Thank you for pushing me and finding me this space to publish my work.

PREFACE

As a scholar of Psychology, in my academic journey, as an Assistant Professor for the past eight years, and lived experiences of 42 years in several different cities in India and also in the USA, I have developed a deep inclination to study the human mind and psyche. Equipped with a natural interest in observing human behavior and uncovering the hidden intricacies behind it, I have spent my life trying to get to the bottom of what makes us think the way we do, what makes us behave the way we do… in short, what makes us human. In order to satisfy my quench for finding answers, I turned to a method of self-reflection that, for me, found a way of expressing itself in poetry.

The process of composing a poem has been a way for me to find answers to my questions about people, and about life in general. As you will see in the poems, most of my poetry is trying to understand an aspect of human behavior, or is a poetic commentary of the way our mind churns experiences within it, in order to come to an understanding of who we are as a person. In my poems, I have tried to address both thoughts and feelings that often lead us to contemplation. I do not propose to provide answers. I just intend to give people a little more of something to think about.

I believe in letting my poems speak for themselves, as they are a way in which I wish for my mind to connect with others. I hope I am able to adequately express myself. I hope I am able to give you something to think about.

Enjoy the experience!

Dr. Kakul Hai

The Shadow

It creeps up
Somewhere in the middle of the night
Catching you unawares
As you imagine a ghastly sight
It numbs your mind
And it tightly clenches your heart
But it's not alone
It has looming anxiety as its counterpart
You look for a reason
But find none to explain
Because others are constantly telling you
That it's just a figment of your imaginative brain
But in the deepest recesses of your mind
You know that it is true
Like the hint of dark clouds appearing
In the sky that should otherwise be a clear blue
I want us to be cautious
But nobody wants to listen to me
They'd rather be blind to the signs
And they leave me alone to just let me be
To some it is obvious
Those who can plainly read the cue
And they are right in being fearful
But alas, those people are, but, just a few
The informed ones shout from the rooftops
But their warnings fall onto deaf ears
Despite the fact that it has been happening

For a number of the past few years
What will it take to make people take notice
If not for themselves, then for their children's
sake
Because the biggest question today is…
Into what kind of doomed future will I tomorrow
awake?

Nature Belittled

Parched earth
Cloudless Sky
From a desolate corner
Emerges a faint cry
Drowned by a thud
Of a fallen tree
Nature has become a corpse
As far as he can see
Green forests lie bare
The stream has changed its course
The sun blazes down upon him
As a punishment for bearing no remorse
The little boy is kneeling
Asking for forgiveness from this earth
To return to him his Mother Nature
From whose womb he has taken birth
He's hoping and he's praying
To be at God's altar
Only to beg and plead for
One tiny drop of water
While all around is the deafening echo
Of the clear yet muffled cry
What have I done to deserve this...
Why, why, why?

Fleeting-ness

That fleeting thought
Lingering on
Holding tight
Keeping all senses entwined,
Born out of a spark
Arising from the shadows
The depths
Taking shape in the abyss of the mind.
Engulfing the self
Permeating the soul
Blurring the vision
Its blaring sound
Slighting the touch
It breathes in the scent unknown.
A sweet harmony
Cacophony of melodies
Arriving on tip-toe,
It teases
It flirts
It taunts
It plays
It reminds…
To look the other way.
A known stranger
Hesitantly welcomed
Suspected of familiarity

It is, alas, just a déjà vu.
I close my eyes
To shut it out
To bathe it in darkness
To extinguish its flicker.
And then,
As I reopen my eyes
I see
That pure light has changed its color

The Guide

Soaring high
As it takes flight
Unperturbed,
By the lingering sigh
When suddenly creeps up
The shadow,
Cast by the flickering candle light
The halted wings
Tied and clipped
Held in an embrace
Of affection that clings
Disturbed,
Arises yearning to break away
From the dark form
The guardian all along the way
Wish is granted
The candle breathes its last
Extinguishing forever
The shadow of the past
Until the sun rises
Bringing with it anew
Letting it know it will be
One in many, many few
The companion
Always by its side
Not a shadow

But its conscience,
Its ever-faithful guide.

From Winter to Spring

Sunday morning
Sunlight creeps in
Wakes me up from my slumber
From the troubles that sleep within
Why am I feeling like this
As if something ought to end
Today or tomorrow,
For how long should I pretend?
I want to break free
Remove all the shackles
Of these intrusive thoughts
I need to find a way to tackle
Someone once said
Live each day like there's no tomorrow
This someone's take on life
Can I for a while borrow…
No, says my mind
This has to absolutely stop
No more thinking this or that
From my head it has to drop
So what if this morning
Has proven to be a difficult one
By the end of the day
I promise to get something extraordinary done
Right now I tell myself
That here is how it goes…

From this moment on
I will let go of my woes
For in my hand it lies
How I want today to be
Even if it is a challenge
Only the good will I see
But, hold on
I hope it doesn't mean
That I'm in denial
Of how my life has been
No, once again is the answer
To this, yet again, troubling thought
Bringing about a change
Is what it is all about
And a worthwhile change
Is what I will bring
Because remember,
After a cold winter
What follows is a glorious spring

Quietness

Quiet days
Can make the mind go astray
Thinking thoughts
That you wish would go away
These thoughts
Engage you in self-reflection
They give you insight
Into what is your life's perception
Life, it seems
Goes on like you're on a roll
But then you realise
You're just caught up in daily rigmarole
Yesterday you were cheerful
Today you're a little sad
And the expectation of tomorrow
Is driving you insanely mad
Why is it that we always expect
Tomorrow to be better than today
Forgetting that today actually was
So much better than yesterday
The sadness that I'm feeling now
Is because of having to let go
Of what you had yesterday
Will you have it tomorrow, you just never know
Living in the past, or living in the future
The problem with both is

That you forgot about today
For which you have to remind yourself this -
That yesterday was, and tomorrow will be
But today is all you have in hand
In the present moment
It's like walking on slippery sand
If you don't focus on your gait
You'll slip hard on the muddy floor
And no matter how much you want
Things will never be like they were before
So make sure to live today
Like there is no tomorrow
That is the only way
To lift up the mind from the present sorrow
Don't worry too much
Of which direction life is going in
Because today is the best day
And the best moment your life has ever been

Beacon of Light

Some days…
It slowly creeps up
The darkness within
Unexpected, unwanted
As if it wanted a free reign
A longing
A lingering desire
For expression
For expulsion
For resolution
For closure
Was I prepared for it?
No
But perhaps deep down
The time was right
For it to surface
To force me to confront
To acknowledge
To accept
To get in touch
With my core
With my inner being
Which was broken
To save itself
From shattering into irreparable pieces
It was my inner soul
Looking for reparation

Wanting to be healed
So I faced it
Accepted it
Acknowledged it
Embraced it
Soothed it
Calmed it down
Gave it a warm hug
And that did its magic!
My inner being was resurrected
It was a new me
Stronger than before
So yes,
Some days can be tough
You're fighting a lonely battle
But what you realise
Is you're not really alone
You have yourself
With you always
Carrying you on your own shoulders
Guiding you through life
So now
I trust
And I have faith
In myself as my own lighthouse
So now I can shine on
And be a beacon of light
Holding and guiding myself
Always and whenever!

Nature's Song

Staring out of the window
Sitting desolately, she let out a heavy sigh
Spending one more day by myself
She resolved to give it another try
Just then, she heard a rustling sound
And as if as an answer to a prayer
The trees began swaying to the beat of wind
Reassuring her that someone up there, did
indeed care
One after another, the tiny raindrops fell
And the clouds began singing a song in unison
And listening closely to the song lyrics
She realized, to be cheerful, they were giving
her a reason
Then came the thunder and lightning
Making her jump up with joy, like a little child
With a huge smile, she let herself out
And threw herself into the lap of nature
Like that child that has gone wild
So what if there were no people around
In this space, she felt immensely free
Because all she needed with her was Mother
Nature
Who always allowed her to be, truly and
completely, ME
So without a moment's hesitation

She embarked upon her favorite rain dance
Because who knew whether this moment would
come again
And there was no way she would let go of this
chance
The wind was now her instrument
And the rain provided the melody
And the rhythm they created together
Made for the best kind of musical parody
And even though she knew this was transitory
That the wind and rain would soon depart
But from now on she would never feel alone
Because this nature's song would forever be in
her heart

Victor's Cry

Deep in the recesses of the mind
Lie a set of conflicting thoughts
One of belief, the other of doubt
Between which I sometimes find myself caught
It makes me struggle
It tells me to compromise
It disturbs me, it jostles my inside
And all this while,
It also catches me by surprise
For I thought I had grown up
I thought I had seen it all
But this internal strife
Is actually a wake-up call
That no matter how much you experience
No matter how much you go through
There will always be a part of you left
That never really fully grew
And that part is what you focus on
That part is what you have to explore
Don't suppress it, don't ignore it
Otherwise it will always make you implore
So on the days you feel challenged
And you don't feel so okay
Let the feeling freely flow
Don't try to keep it at bay
Because underneath all the struggle

Lie all the issues that are troubling you
But after digging through the surface
You will find the strength to fight it too
And eventually you will emerge as a winner
One who never stops to try
Because then your doubts will fade away
And you can finally yell out a true victor's cry!

To BE

There is a space within me that I often retreat
into
Where I meet a part of me, that gets expressed in
instances that are very few
Here I am able to think and with myself debate
And the comfort that I feel within makes many
of my worries abate
I sometimes wonder why is it that I cannot stay
here all of the time
Where time and space are nobody else's, they
are simply all mine
I can have all that I want, I don't have to share
And the best thing is, that about nobody else I
am obliged to care
But then, a little thought that strikes me
Is whether do I really want to be and feel all that
free?
No attachments, no expectations, just a carefree
life
Isn't that the best kind of life, where there is no
kind of strife?
No struggles, no frustrations of trying to make
ends meet
The only thing that matters is that peace is there
for me to greet?

Some call it soul-searching, which is essential
for me to do
Because by seeking out my soul purpose I will
eventually find my Self too
But...
Like I just said, there always crops up a but
And I'm told that from my mind I have to
forever make this thought cut
It's easier said than done, or is it really so?
Will I ever be able to shrug off the baggage that
I need to let go?
Will there ever be a time that I will be able to
release the stress?
Perhaps Be-Who-I-Am is what I'm supposed to
upon myself impress
But there's a part of me, that wants to live for
another
And not able to live up to another's
expectations, is my life's major bother
Caught in this conflict, I'm constantly looking
for a release
Sometimes asking God, to provide me with a
solution please
The solution, finally it did arrive
That from within myself only would the answer
derive
Go within, introspect, engage with your soul
Because the truth lies there only, it's the only
way you will become whole

Seek your truth within yourself, it will take you
to places
That before unknown territory, where you will
find all the traces
Of who you are, and where you actually belong
And you will discover that you knew who you
were all along
So take that leap of faith, on this account you
can completely trust me
For this knowing is what will finally set you free
To not just DO, but to be yourself, to just BE!

Stranger in the City

I'm a stranger in the city
But I don't need your pity
I'm writing a new chapter of my life
Yet another story,
Of some triumph and some strife

Something new, everywhere that I look
Some new learnings, some reassurances…
Made a part of me stay, but another part of me it
took
Everywhere, my inner strength I have to take
Because some experiences have made my
essence shake

A story here, another story there
Abound with idiosyncratic characters
everywhere
Different perspectives, different attitudes
But none boring you with repeated platitudes

Some new friendships, some new battles
Some deliberately attempting to make you rattle
Each experience teaches me something new
Even though instances of familiarity are
relatively few

But would I have it any other way?
Absolutely not,
Even if being an outsider is the price that I pay

HOW?

How is it that I can make my life a success?

Have I been born with inborn talents that for
success are required?
Or are all skills through practice and
perseverance acquired?
Is it the doing of luck and the sweet smile of
fortune?
Or can I create for myself moments of
opportune?
Do I put myself out there or wait to be
discovered?
Or how else will what I have to offer be
uncovered?
Are opportunities supposed to come knocking
on my door?
Or do I have to mark a path for myself on the
rugged floor?
Do I become a risk-taker, and a threat to my own
sanity?
Or continue to have ambitions that might even
defy gravity?
Should I dream on and be brimming with
endless hope?
Or make compromises with reality that will help
me to cope?

Should I listen to others and learn from their
experience?
Or is it only through myself that I will find my
deliverance?
Should I look up to others and find sources of
inspiration?
Or will the reality of un-achievability only cause
indignation?
Is it true that some people can do whatever they
want?
Or do they simply just choose to not do what
they can't?
Can I be the one who decides what I want to do?
Or are there other powers that decide what I can
and must do?
Are there actually endless chances that I can for
myself avail?
Or is there a set track I have to follow, or my life
train will derail?

Is it ever possible to gain access to everything?
How does one ever really manage to achieve
anything?

Wrong Door

25

Sometimes we keep knocking on the wrong door
Never questioning what we are doing it for
It may seem that is what we desire
And not getting it makes our hopes retire
However, on the side is a small window, which
we fail to tender
Letting in a ray of hope, however slender
Unnoticeable, when the days are bright and
shiny
And the effect of the small ray of sunshine is
tiny
It is only in our darkest days of gloom
That the tiny ray of light causes our hopes to
once again bloom
If only earlier towards the window we had
turned our face
We would have found ourselves in our rightful
place
Because when the door we want to open is
firmly locked
It is behind that small window that our
happiness is stocked

When...

When,
There are more backward glances than looking
straight into the eyes
And every time you speak, a blooming
connection prematurely dies

When,
The outward stillness holds more anguished
ripples than collective calm
And the sweetness of the laughter no longer
serves as a balm

When,
The nearness in between adds to the mind's
cacophony
Because the words spoken only play a
bittersweet symphony

When,
There are overladen silences and empty spoken
words
Which softly and ruggedly tug away at the
heart's chords

When,
The heart's desires no longer match outward
action
And the mind begins to fear the tongue's
unpredictable reaction

When,
The masks you put on lie piled up on the shelf
You know it's time to walk away… from
yourself

Reverberations

I WON to ensure the continuation of my reign
I LOST the chance to introduce a slight flavor of
change

I WON for myself a glorious present and future
I LOST the anticipation of victory lurking
around the corner

I WON with good fortune flowing in full gear
I LOST out on measuring my inner strength by
facing my worst fear

I WON and made people swell with pride
I LOST the opportunity to discover which of
them would accompany me down the slide

I WON and became who I am, as was destined
by thee
I LOST the serendipitous opportunity of
becoming who I could also be.

Serendipity

I always wished there would come a day
When I would confidently be able to say
For everything that happens there are always
reasons
As definite as there are, in a year, four seasons
And figuring them out would not be a stroke of
genius
All it would require is an insight, profound and
serious
And then it so happened that this thinking of
time
Held strongly by me over the passage of time
Was irrevocably challenged in a single and brief
moment
The experience of which brought great
existential torment
I searched within myself, in a state of emotional
seclusion
And finally came to an unexpected conclusion:
That several instances which have shaped my
identity
Can only be explained by, plain and simple,
serendipity.

In the End...

The pear-shaped raindrops falling down from the
sky
Are signalling to me, to give it a try
As unexpected as is this winter rain
With its balmy quality, washing away all the
pain.
On this cold, rainy, winter day
What it wants is for me to say
Whatever it is that life throws my way
I will embrace it gladly, come what may
Because every experience with it brings a new
learning
And to evolve as a person is what I am yearning
So from this day forward, I take a vowNever to
life's challenges surrender with a bow
I will rise to the occasion, facing it with all my
might
Because, I believe, that in the end, everything
will be all right.

The Launch

31

Raising my head on hearing the echoes running
through the hall
Sounds of pitter-patter and tick-tock
I rose from my chair to inquire about the drop or
fall
Peering out, I saw that the sail was set to launch

Invincible

There was once a time when I felt invincible
And every moment of my life was memorable
But it was only when with my vulnerability I
came face to face
That I was able to accept the meaning of my
existence with grace
Now, the wish that I have for my life is..
To be full of moments just like this:
Moments of passion, sincerity, and dedication,
felt today and tomorrow
And as a human being, greatness will on its own
follow.

A Warrior

She lived like a warrior, conquering all kinds of
strife
To all of us she seemed much larger than life
But although she appeared brighter than
sunshine
Secretly, it was for simple affection that she did
pine
Every time I look at her, it is all too clear
That despite the many things in her life she has
to fear
She'll brave life's challenges with all of her
might
She'll always be a woman, who stands tall in her
own right

Destiny's Child

He was born, not with his mouth holding a silver
spoon
Instead, destined to live a life of fortitude,
While others are attempting to find routes of
escape
He manages to build an oasis in the midst of the
fray,
I am an idea borne out of an unyielding mind, he
says
I am, albeit of a different kind, after all destiny's
child.

Time

*For my 7-year-old Londoner niece, who said she
has no time because she is too busy opening her
birthday presents and reading her school
books...*

We tend to treat the concept of personal time
Akin to something that is dozen a dime
But in truth,
Trying to find TIME to do things is like being at
a stage
When you are trying to fit too many words on a
single page
So even though being "busy" is an essential
imperative
Take care that it does not become your entire
life's narrative

Regardless,
With you, my lovely, I am always gonna try
Every single time, even after I say goodbye

State of Mind

Too much darkness
Too much emotional pain
I wonder about my life
I wonder what is there to gain?

Days are gloomy
There is constant mental stress
What is the lesson to be learned here?
What are these experiences trying to impress?

I know there is a way out
I know things will change
But until that happens
I will seem to myself as someone very strange

Today, it may be distressing
As more days than not are rough
An insight I can gain is
That I am internally very tough

So yes, right now it's difficult
And the unpleasant outweighs the good
Regardless, there's scope for improvement
This I have very well understood

So, I will carry on

Striving to do my best
And the universe will conspire
And put everything unpleasant to rest

But one thing to remember is
That even if I'm not doing well
I will forgive myself for slip-ups
And on my own faults I will not dwell

It's okay to make mistakes
It's okay to sometimes fail
Through all this, I have to tell myself
That eventually the strength in me will prevail

So, the bottom line is this:
No matter how badly some people treat you
You have to, first and foremost, like your own
self
That is the most important survival cue
For you have to invest in yourself

So, chin up!
And get down to the grind
They will say whatever they want about you
Just, never-mind, never-mind

Free!

Staring out of his gilded cage
He dreamt of flying free and unbound
Yet,
On the day of his release
He found his feet were firmly rooted in the
ground.

Thinking

Think of
Pleasant memories to keep you company
Vivid fantasies to keep you entertained
Mindfulness to remove all agony
Meditate, and peace of mind is attained

For Noreen…

She's sweet, and for her age she's
extraordinarily kind
She doesn't let us know, but she's got a brilliant
mind
Even as a baby, she was tuned into my mood
And through her baby love, even then she made
me feel soothed
When she came to know that she was going to
have a baby brother
She declared that he was her own baby, a special
person in her life like no other
When her mother was sick, she would offer to
give her a cuddle
Opening up her pitara of love, she would encase
her into a warm bubble
It's a surprise as to how much she seems to
underestimate herself
But deep down I know she has a conviction of
immense belief in her own self
You may not know this, but at just age 11 she is
extremely wise
And in a person so young, such humility catches
you by surprise
She is all this, and so much more
She is a person you cannot help loving and adore

So, my darling, remain as you are, and I cannot
wait to see you grow
And always remember this,
I love you and will always be there for you,
Supporting you as you go ahead in life and
achieve things more and more

For my best friend…

During a year that has been rough,
He has diligently looked after me
And with all his kindness bestowed,
He has made me feel comfortable and free

In the times when I was troubled,
He listened to me with a lot of care
And with his reassuring presence
He helped me pass a challenging time by
holding it up to a dare

Yet, despite him being the provider,
He also has a need to be taken care of
And what he doesn't realise is this:
The more he takes care of people around him
The larger becomes his group of grateful kin

So, my dear, keep being who you are,
And always remember, that on the days you feel
exhausted and overwhelmed
All of us are there for you, none of us are too far

As long as you are in people's thoughts,
You are going to be absolutely fine
And I hope you will always remember

That you are a very important person, who I will
always cherish as mine

43

Missing

Even though such instances are quite few
And despite everything else that you always do
I still feel that something major is missing
And to find that something I am always fishing
I seem to think that there is something missing
between you and me
But, on thinking about it, I find that in my mind
I don't feel free
Free enough to feel that you will always be there
That even though sometimes you don't respond,
it doesn't mean that you don't care
I realised that if I care, I shouldn't cage you in
my expectations
Because then you will just go along to keep up
the pretentions
In order to satisfy me, you should not have to try
so much
That one day you get exhausted, because I made
you feel such
Nobody should have to prove they care, over
and over again
And if I cared for you, I should not make you do
that, again and again
So the one thing that I realised is thus
That I shouldn't make things so difficult for the
both of us

That whatever my problems are I should keep
them to me
So that you don't feel fettered, and instead can
feel free
You should feel that when with me, you can be
whatever it is you want to be
And not feel the burden of living up to the
expectations that have been set by me
So feel free, my friend, to be whoever you
actually are
No more trouble will I give you, that is my
promise to you at this midnight hour

Birthday Wish

My little angel whispered in my ear
That something special was going to happen this
year
As you grow a year older, and become a bit
more wiser
Towards your destiny you are going to move one
huge step closer
This year, you will find new ways of being
yourself
And not just others, but you too will say, "I am
proud of myself"
In your life, you will begin to pave your own
path
A life will begin, which from your desired
choices would have been carved
No more being what others want you to be
Coz already the roots are deep enough, now's
the time to add blossoms to your life's tree
The seeds were planted long ago, now's the time
for them to flower
For you to charge ahead towards success, with
full-on power!
And do you know why this year all of this will
happen?
Because now you are strong enough to never let
your spirit dampen

So whatever curveball life will from now on
throw
Your sensitivity and wisdom will counter it, and
make you further grow
And in addition, one thing I am sure that you
will always keep in mind
Is that no matter what are the challenges, you
will always remain kind

So, my dear, this is my prayer for you...
That this year you are going to finally feel free
Because a new life is going to begin... that is
your birthday wish from me

Tomorrow

The bittersweet memories that suddenly haunt
you one day
As if to check up on you whether you are doing
okay
To see that when the past catches up with you
Are you able to still grasp onto the present too
I'm not the same person that I was a day before
Despite yesterday's emotion today it's doing an
encore
Yesterday I was frail, I let it consume me
But today, from its upheaval, I'm feeling
relatively free
Today I am stronger, and it's all because of you
You, who amongst the crowd, counts as one of
the few
The you who always lifts me from my
memories' sorrow
That you is the me that I will be tomorrow

Inner Strength

When the only voice that speaks to you
Is the one that is coming from inside of you
You console yourself that it's just a test
And soon things will turn out for the best
For sure, the silence around is deafening
And it is only your own voice to which you can
be listening
Just have to remember one thing,
That though everyone from your life might right
now be gone
It is your own inner strength that will make you
go on

Always

Time is short
But life is long
So live in a way
That you remain healthy and strong

Relationships are transient
But make connections that are deep
And make sure all your close ones
In your life you will forever keep

But, love, that lasts forever
And it lives beyond your lifetime too
And remember to tell those people
That no matter what, I will always love you!

Cobwebs of the Mind

In these times of uncertainty
The only thing I'm sure about
Is that I'll emerge out of it a different person
The kind that is not afraid
And instead always finds a way around

So to all the people out there
This is what I have to say
This is the time to conquer your fears
And remove the cobwebs from your mind
Because at the end, it will all be okay
But only if,
To yourself you are kind

A Walk In The Clouds

*From the forest to the mountains... This one was
written while in Mussoorie/Landour in June, 2014*

It appears the heavens have descended upon the
earth
Sneaking upon me as they smoothly glide across
the hearth
I take a deep breath, inhaling the distinct scent
of the purity of nature
Brought along by the dew-laden clouds, dancing
on the expanse pasture
My eyes are sweetly overwhelmed by the
shining glory of the greens
In them I get a glimpse of a cosmic sanctity,
pure and clean
The deafening silence broken by the calls of
chirping crickets
The occasional bark of the guard dogs, fenced
behind the pickets
I make my own music, along the narrow
mountain lanes as I strode
It's the crushing sound of the dried brown leaves
strewn across the road
Accompanying me on my walk are hordes of
colorful butterflies

Who have stolen their hues from the rainbows
adorning the monsoon skies
The sweetness of the nectar sucked from flowers
has got them energized
And they attack me with a vigor that leaves me
mighty surprised
Soon I feel raindrops streaming down my face,
tasting like sugary tears
The thundering clouds signaling the Gods'
throats being cleared
They speak, not with sound, but with lightning
bolts
Brightening up the darkening mountainside with
small bursts of flaming jolts
As the mountains bathe in the heavenly shower,
I stand with open arms
Welcoming the glistening tears of angels, like a
beggar collects alms
I experience an intimacy with nature that tugs at
my heart's strings
Gently nudging at my slumbering soul, an
inherent awakening it brings
The feeling of a still and violently calming
stirring is one of its kind
And it is here alone that I experience such peace
of mind
Oh, the wonder of the mountains, I say
Cradled in the lap of nature, inviting me to
forever stay

Song

When I find myself in times of trouble
When darkness looms,
And of cheerfulness there's no sign or trace
All I need is a thought of you
And I'm immediately transported to my happy
place

You may not be close to me
You may be miles away
But the thought of our memories together
Is enough to make my dark mood sway

The days ahead will be difficult
So here's one promise I need from you
You will always come to my mind as a happy
thought
Even if our chats are far between and few

And in return my promise to you is
That every time we find ourselves apart
I will be for you that sweet symphony
Which will be a song you can forever carry in
your heart

Togetherness

55

As she sat, lost in her thoughts
One feeling kept nagging her heart
Of hopelessness, in this time of crisis
For how much longer were they going to be
apart

They were separated by hundreds of miles
But had promised to stay connected
By keeping each other in their thoughts
They would keep one another protected

Then she realised that it really didn't matter
Whether they were far or they were near
For as long as there were memories of
togetherness
The absence was irrelevant, of this she was very
clear

New Year

This New Year,
Make sure you see the light
Everyday dispelling the night;
Catch a glimpse of the bloom
Bringing fragrance to your room;
Breathe in the fullness of life
And cancel out all reason for a strife;
Let only kind words in your ears ring
For much joy and happiness they do bring;
Let only pleasant memories fill your mind
That with a beautiful stroke you have signed.

Whisperings of the Mind

57

It tells me to let go… so that I can grasp,
The fleeting thought that sits
On the horizon of my mind's I
Reach out with my phantom imagination
To let it alight,
To let it fly sky-high
In order to float free
Away from the trappings that exist…
In the whisperings of my mind

Kehne Do

Kehne do unhe jo kehna hai
Humein fark nahi padta
Sahi aur galat ka antar
Humein bhi khoob hai pata

Nafrat karne wale bahut hain duniya mein
Karna hai bus khud pe yakeen
Chalte raho apne sach ki raah pe
Yahi banaayega tumhe auron se haseen

Ho sakta hai paaoge khud ko kabhi kabhi akela
Koi baat nahi, bas datte raho
Karte raho khud se pyaar
Nahin jhuka sakta koi mujhe,
Bas yahi khud se kehte raho

Maano apni galti jahan par ho
Aur lao apne mein sudhaar
Lekin apne saath naainsaafi hone
Se hamesha karo inkaar

Hila de khud pe se apna yakeen
Yahin bas nahi hone dena hai
Do log kya ho gaye tumhaare khilaaf
Tavajjo apne ek us sahaare pe rakhna hai

Jo jaante nahi tumhe
Woh karenge bahut saari baatein
Chodo, kehne do unhe jo kehna hai
Kyun kharaab karein hum apni raatein

Khud ke sach pe rakho bharosa
Haan, hai yeh mushkil, magar aasaan bhi
Himmat rakho, chaahe kitni nafrat aaye
Tumhari zindagi mein kabhi-kabhi

Toh aaj bolo khud se
Ki nahi hila sakta koi mujhko
Kar lo jo karna chahte hoi, aye zindagi
Nahi haar maan ni mujhe,
Yahi kahoongi har baar khud ko

Koshish

Tum itna jo koshish karte ho
Samajhne ki mujhe
Kahin ek din thak na jao
Ho jao tum thode se bujhe-bujhe

Bana li hai zindagi tumne doosron ke baare mein
Rehte ho hamesha maujood sabke liye
Bas ek baat aati hai mann mein
Kya kisi aur ne kiya hai yeh tumhare liye?

Bas yahi fikr sataati hai mere dost
Ki sabke liye maujood hone ki wajah se
Kahin bhool na jao khud ko
Kho na jao tum kahin khud se

Magar phir main sochti hoon
Yehi hai tumhari sabse badi taaqat
Kabhi akela nahin paoge tum khud ko
Kyunki inhi karmo se banegi tumhari sunehri
kismat

Mera dost

Ek mera dost hai
Jo karta hai sabse pyaar
Aur sabse achchi baat hai
Woh karta hai pyaar ka izhaar

Itna pyaara, itna maasoom
Hai woh ki lagta hai mujhe darr
Ki dil na toot jaaye uska ek din
Kyunki sab log aise nahin hain magar

Yeh jo uski baat hai bahut achchi
Is se fyada hota hai sabko
Yeh sab ke sab hain special
Aisa mehsoos karata hai woh in logon ko

Toh mera darr hai yehi
Ki milta kya hai use iske badle?
Kyunki in mein se bahut saare log
Hain andar se thode se khokhle

Magar yeh jo mera dost hai
Woh maanta hai yeh baat…
Ki pyaar hota hai khul kar baantne ko
Yahi hai zindagi ki sabse khoobsurat saugaat

Ab main kya karun

Kar sakti hoon bas yehi dua
Ki khushi dene mein mile use dugni khushi
Aur kabhi toote na uska dil,
Kyunki kisi aur ne na uske saath kabhi aisa kiya

Lekin ek baat ka hai mujhe yakeen
Ki yeh mera darr niklega galat ek din
Aur use milega koi bahut pyaar karne wala
Jo na reh paayega uske bin

Toh mere dost
Karte raho sabse aisa hi pyaar
Kyunki tumhari zindagi mein hain
Humare jaise bhi sachche yaar

Woh Din

Lag raha hai phir se aa rahe hain woh din
Jab rehna padega aap sab logon ke bin
Kaisa hai yeh waqt, jo badal hi nahi raha
Jo kal hua tha, woh hi aaj bhi hai ho raha
Is waqt mein hai bahut tanhayee
Jo la rahi hai khud pe bahut kathinayi
Phir se ban na padega aatmanirbhar
Jab rehna padega akele poore din bhar
Chalo din toh nikal jaata hai, mushkil hoti hai
raat
Lekin khush kismat hoon main, kyunki roz ho
jaati hai aap se baat
Toh phir itna kya sochna, guzar jaayega yeh
waqt bhi aasaani se
Kyunki duur hi sahi, aap hain mere saath
Ghar pe na sahi, lekin mere dil ke hain paas

Doosra Din

64

Aaj lag raha hai ki zindagi mein koi mazaa nahi
hai
Bhatak sa raha hoon, koi raah nahi hai
Kuch khoya-khoya sa hoon main aaj
Jaise ki nahi pata chal paa raha hai apne andar
ka koi raaz
Khud ko bol raha hoon ki hai yeh bhavna sirf aaj
hi ke liye
Kal hai ek doosra din, bahut saare kaam karne
ke liye

Zehen

65

Chal raha hai aaj kal kuch zehen mein
Kuch hain uljhane, jo aa rahi nahin hain samajh
mein
Aati nahi neend jaldi raaton mein
Aur nikal jaata hai din bas yahan wahan ki soch
mein
Waise kar toh rahe hain hum bahut saara kaam
Ki jaldi se nikal jaata hai din, aur aa jaati hai
shaam
Lekin phir bhi lagta hai jo kiya hai woh hai kam
Kyunki aaj kal kuch khoye huye se hain hum

Pal

Woh aaj hain, par nahi hain kal
Unka saath likha tha bas kuch hi pal
Par un kuch hi palon mein woh de gaye aisi
yaadein
Jinke baare mein hum kar sakte hain zindagi
bhar baatein
Woh pal the itne haseen, bhare the itni saari
khushiyon se
Aur ab yaad rakhna hai un khushiyon ko, jo hai
judaai se pare
Kyunki woh sikha gaye humein kya hota hai
mohabbat karna
Ek nanhi si jaan se, jisne sikhaya humein
dukhon se ubharna
Uske saath ne dikhaaya ki kaun hain hum
Toh kya hua ki hamara saath likha tha bahut hi
kam
Toh faisla kiya hai ki judaai pe hum nahi
royenge
Aur na hi apne andar koi kami ko khojenge
Aur unke saath se apne aap ko jo hai paaya... bas
usi ke baare mein hamesha sochenge

Dil Nadaan

Jab kabhi bhi dil ghabra raha ho
Socho un logon ke baare mein
Jo parwah karte hain tumhari
Aur hote hain pareshan tumhare baare mein

Kya karna chahiye unhe pareshan
Jab khud mein ho kuch kashmakash?
Ya akele hi sehna chahiye sab kuch
Kyunki khud hi duur kar sakte hain hum yeh
kashmakash?

Dilaani hai khud ko itni himmat
Ki chahe jaise bhi ho halaat
Muh pe hamesha rakhni hai muskaan
Aur zubaan pe rakhni hai mithaas

Jo aapke saath hai unhe rakhna hai apne paas
Na isliye kyunki woh hain aapke liye pareshan
Magar isliye kyunki yeh dekh kar ki aap hain
pareshan
Woh jaante hain ki is silsile ko bhi aap kar lenge
aasaani se paar

Ghabarahat

Aaj dil kuch ghabara sa raha hai
Jaane kis kism ka maajrah chaaya hua hai
Chaaron taraf toot rahi hai logon ki himmat
Aur woh tabse haath baandhkar sirf yeh nazaara
dekhe jaa raha hai

Koi nahi kar raha hai kuch
Kyunki kisi ke bas mein nahi hai karne ko kuch
bhi?
Kya hum tab bhi nahi karenge kuch
Jab hoga shikaar humara koi dost-yaar bhi?

Kuch kehte hain ki hum likhte hain apni kismat
khud hi
And kuch kehte hain ki likhi-likhayi aati hai
hamari kismat
Kya hai sach, yeh jaanti nahi hoon main
Bas itna pata hai
Kisi ki kismat mein nahi likhi hai zindagi ki is
taraf ki baerukhi

Bhoolna

Kabhi-kabhi dil chahta hai ki duniya-daari
chhod doon
Magar phir lagta hai ekdum se darr, ke apni
zaroorat ko na main kahin kho doon
Lekin lagta hai yeh bhi
Ki jo hai zaroori woh rahega hamesha hi mere
paas
Hai woh dil ka mere ek tukda, jo rahega
hamesha bahut hi khaas
Uske hone se hai zindagi mein bahaar, isliye hai
woh zaroori
Mushkil ho jaayegi us din, jis din woh ban
jaayega meri majboori
Woh hoga us din, jab main rakhoonga khud ko
us se pehle
Aur mujhe hai pata yeh bhi, ki khud ko paaungi
tab main bilkul akele
Yeh bhi jaanta hoon main ki hoon main ek kali
jisko abhi hai khilna
Aur mere khilne ke liye tha hum dono ko is
zindagi mein milna
Abhi toh hum mile hain, hai lamba raasta
humein saath mein tay karna
Chhoota yeh saath, toh bahut bada jurmaana
hoga mujhe bharna

Chahoonga main tumhe rakhna hamesha apne
bahut kareeb
Lekin zindagi mein kya hoga, mujhe pata nahi
kya hai mera naseeb
Ho sakta hai ki meri zindagi bahut zyada
masroof ho jaaye
Bhool na jaana mujhe, agar kabhi-kabhi hamaari
baat na ho paaye...

Masla

Yeh kya masla hai zindagi ka
Kitni jaldi guzar jaata hai lamha mutaasir hone
ka
Us pal se jismein hai zindadilli
Kyunki masroofiyat se laga chuke hain hum
dillagi
Bhool jaate hain hum mahsoos karna woh ehsaas
Jab hota hai zindagi ka sahi maayna humaare
paas
Jab ek gaz ki hi hoti hai doori
Lekin use naa thaam paana ban jaati hai humaari
majboori
Lagta hai ki khul ke naa jee paana hi hai
humaara karm
Baawaajood iske sajaate hain hum apni zindagi
mein bahut saare bhram
Shaayad kehte hain asal ki zindagi jeena isi ko
Jahan bahut kuch khona hi hai naseeb hum ko

Zindagi

72

Unki maujoodgi se milti thi bahut saari khushi
Lekin aaj unke jaane par main hoon nahi dukhi
Kyunki asal mein ab hogi unki zindagi shuru
Aur unki anokhi kismat unko le jaayegi bahut hi
duur
Khushi hogi jaankar ki unki zindagi mein bahaar
aayi
Koi gham nahi judai ka,
Kyunki ab zindagi unke liye khoob saare haseen
tohfe hai laayi

Main

Achaanak se man mein aaya yeh khayaal
Ki kya main sach mein jaanti hoon khud ko?
Ya karni hai abhi aur mehnat
Apne aap ko pehchaan ne ki mujh ko?

Kya koi batayega mujhe
Ki main kaun hoon?
Lekin kisi aur ke bataane se bhi
Kya mil paayega mere man ko sukoon?

Talaashna hoga mujhe khud hi
Mere is sawaal ka jawaab
Uthaana hoga mujhe khud hi
Apne upar par se chadha huya yeh naqaab

Jawaab mein dil kehta hai kuch
Aur dimaag kehta hai kuch aur
Khatam karni hai dono ki uljhan
Taaki shuru ho khud ki shakhseeyat ka ek naya
daur

Toh bas thaan liya hai ab
Khud se kar liya hai vaada, aur ek iqraar
Apne aap se hogi mulaqat jald hi
Bas usi lamhe ka hai ab intezaar

Kaun?

Usne poocha mujhse ki main kaun hoon
Kya hain mere khwab, kya hai meri tamanna
Iska jawaab aasaan tha, aur mushkil bhi
Kyunki meri pehchaan ki gehrayi thi bepanah

Main woh hoon jise aap jaante ho
Samjhte ho aur karte ho mahsoos
Lekin mujhme kuch aisa bhi hai
Jise na jaan paane ka ho sakta hai aapko afsoos

Aisa nahi hai ki maine hai kuch chupaaya
Ya rakha hai aapko andhere me
Bas apne aap ka kuch hissa
Rakh liya hai hai khud ke liye, apne hi me

Shaayad ek din ho aapki mulaaqat
Mere us pehlu se jisme mera antarman hai
samaaya
Aur us din humein lag jaayega jaise
Humaare rishte mein ek hai ek naya mod aaya

Rishte

75

Har rishte mein aate hain pal
Jab hoti hain naaraazgiyan
Us pal bhoolna nahi chaahiye woh din
Jinme mehsoos ki thi bahut saari khushiyaan

Agar rishta hai gehra
Toh mahsoos honge har tarah ke jazbaat
Aur jazbaat ki gehrayi hi hai jo aapko le jaayegi
paar
Chaahe jaise bhi hoon hum dono ke haalat

Chaahe pyar ho ya ho naaraazgi
Agar aapko poori karni hai apni kahaani
Bas ek baat ka khayaal rakhna
Ki rishte mein naa ho kisi tarah ki beimaani

Waqt

Waqt par hoti hai nazar
Jab waqt hota hai kam
Aur choot jaane ka waqt ka
Humein hota hai sabse zyada gham

Aao seekh lein hum tarqeeb
Thaam lene ki waqt ko
Kas ke rakheinge apni muthi mein
Taaki nikal jaaye na waqt humare haathon se kal
ko

Kyunki beeta waqt nahi aayega waapas
Aur aane wala waqt nahi kabhi humari pakad
mein
Bas yahi lamha hai jo hai
Guzaaro use is tarah
Jaise lage ki zindagi hai apni hi giraft mein

Guru

Ek tha waqt
Jab tha woh mera guru
Jiski kahi huyi baaton se
Meri soch hoti thi shuru

Usne sikhaaya mujhe bahut kuch
Ki zindagi kaise jeete hain
Ki hamare tajurbe hi hain jo
Hamare kirdaar ko seechte hain

Mujhe laga woh rahega mere saath umr bhar
Jiske saath ki wajah se main kar paongi sab kuch
jhel
Lekin uska chale jaana hi tha
Jo sikha gaya mujhe sambhalna is zindagi ke
sabhi khel

Yeh samajh mein aaya mujhe baad me
Haath chodkar woh ban gaya tha mera saaya
Aur yeh sochkar ki karna hai sab mujhe ab akele
Hai maine khud ko poori tarah samjha, aur hai
paaya

Mujhe laga tha main gum ho jaungi
Zindagi mein uska saath kho kar
Lekin ab mujhe samajh mein aaya

Woh mujhe sikha raha tha, khud par hi hamesha
hona nirbhar

Toh ab aaj hoon main azaad
Kyunki mere khayaal hain ab sirf mere
Aur yahi hain uska diya tohfa mujhe
Ki nahin hai kuch bhi meri azaadgi se pare

Wajah

Jab sochne baithta hoon
Toh lagta hai kal tha bahut khoobsoorat
Jiski wajah se aaj hoon main aisa
Is liye kal ki yaadein hain meri zaroorat

Lekin phir aata hai yeh khayaal
Ki kal jo tha woh toh beet gaya
Jo hai mere paas woh aaj hai
Aaj, jis se hai mera muqaddar juda hua

Aaj main woh hoon
Jo nahi tha main kal
Aur kal main kya hounga
Woh nirbhar hai mere aaj ke har pal par

Isi khayaal se kiya hai ab yeh faisla
Ki ab nahi rakhni hai kal ke beet jaane ki
ghabaraahat
Dekhna hai bas aane wale kal ki or
Mukh pe rakhe huye beete kal ki di huyi
muskuraahat

Baatein

Jab kisi ki kahi baaton se
Chha jaati hai dil mein khamoshi
Tab na chahe koi kar le kitni bhi koshish
Nahi mehsoos hoti hai ehsaas ki madhoshi

Bikhar jaate hain saare khayaal
Ho jaate hain dil ke tukde
Jo nahi jud pate phir kabhi bhi
Chahe jitna bhi koi aur humein lipat kar pyar se
pakde

Yehi sochta hai mann
Kyun ban gaya tha woh itna zaroori
Jab use ban jaana tha aaj
Na khush reh paane ki sabse badi majboori

Phir aata hai ek khayaal
Ki usko chahna tha nahi koi jurm
Kyunki dil todne mein bhi woh de gaya ek sabak
Jo yaad rahega humein apni poori umr

Ab kiya hai yeh faisla, ki tuta toh sirf dil hi hai
Isme koi badi baat nahi
Bikhar gaya hai dil tukdon mein
Lekin phir bhi,

Tukdon mein hi sahi, baste hain abhi bhi jazbaat
wahi

81

Soch

Roz sochte hain hum
Karni hain tumse kuch baatein
Magar kaise kahein, yahi sochne mein
Nikal jaati hain saari raatein

Kabhi lagta hai khul kar bol dein
Kyunki tumko bataana hai zaroori
Magar phir sochte hain na bata paane to peeche
Hogi koi na koi sachchi majboori

Lekin kya bolne ki sach mein hai zaroorat?
Bina kahe kya tumhe nahi pata chal jaata?
Kya ankahi baaton ko samajhna
Tumhe sach mein nahi aata?

Shaayad maine hi lagaayi huyi hai ummeed
Jo kabhi na poori ho paaye
Bas is na samajhne ke chakkar mein
Kahin hamari kahaani hi na khatam ho jaaye

Toofan

Jaise ki mere andar utha toofan ho gaya ho kuch
kam
Kyunki khud se baatein bahut saari karne ke
baad
Filhaal chup ho gaya ho mera mann

Jaise raat ke andhere mein ho jaata hai ghana
sannata
Jab ek patti bhi naa hile
Aur naa jaag raha ho koi jo mujhe sataata

Jaise ek tez dopahar ke baad aa jaati hai jo
shaam
Aur din bhar ki hulchul to baad
Ab nahi rehta karne ko zyada kuch kaam

Jaise mehsoos hota hai akelapan
Jab peene ke baad chadh jaati hai behoshi
Ab aisa lagne raha hai ki
Chaa gayi hai iss duniya mein khamoshi

Khayal

Ek khayaal mujhe roz satata hai
Jaise bekhayaali ke din ho rahe hain kam
Kahin bhool na jaun main aazaad rehna
Bade hone ka bas yahi hai gham

Aaj choti si baat se mil jaati hai badi khushi
Kya kal chhoti-chhoti naaqamiyan hi kar dengi
mujhe dukhi?

Aaj doston ke saath bitaayi ek shaam mein jo
milte hain maze
Kya kal apni masroofiyat mein wahi dost bhool
jaayenge mujhe?

Aaj Maa ki ek daant se jo hosh udd jaatein hain
mere
Kya kal zindagi sikhaayegi koi sabak jo hoga
Maa ki daant se bhi pare?

Aaj Papa ki di huyi salaah se nahi badhkar hai
kuch bhi
Kya kal lene honge faisle apne dam par mujhe
hi?

Aaj apne pehle pyaar ke khayaal se jo aa jaati
hai muh pe muskurahat

Kya kal woh pyaar rahega mere saath, jo duur
kare meri saari ghabarahat?

Aise hi khayaal roz satate hain mujhe
Kya bada hona hai mujhe?
Ya reh sakta hoon main bachcha hi
Zindagi ke har din ke saanjh aur savere?

Jazbaat

Bina ruke bina thame
Aise behte gaye mere jazbaat
Jaise jala diya ho kisi ne ek diya
Jisne di mujhe roshni ek kaali andheri raat

Mujhe laga hogi bahut musibat
Thak jaunga main, haar jaunga main
Lekin mujhe kya pata tha is silsile mein
Khud hi ko paa jaunga main

Toh phir kya tha
Hichkichaahat ko phook maari maine
Aur ab toh yeh aalam hai
Us safar par nikal pada hoon main
Jis par sirf ehsaas ke bal par chalna jaari kar diya
hai maine

Hum Tum

Jab poori duniya naa jaan paayi
Tab usne hi samjha mujhe
Naa aaya woh doosron ki baaton mein
Naa khud ko usne hone diya ulajhna mujhme

Woh sahi, main galat
Aisi thi naa kabhi hamaare beech kashmakash
Itni samajh toh thi hum dono mein
Ki naa kholne pade humein apne apne tarkash

Ek samjhauta tha,
Ki tu tu hai, aur main main hoon
Hum dono naa the ek duje se pare
Aur is hi ek wajah se, apne rishtey mein
Hum ek doosre ki nazron mein kabhi nahi gire

Yaadein

Yaad nahi aisa koi pal mujhe
Jab yaad na kiya ho maine tujhe
Jab socha na maine ki tu ruk jaaye
Tu tham jaaye, tu thahar jaaye
Taaki is pal ko main qaid kar loon
Yeh pal, jiske aage mera naseeb bhi jhuk jaaye

Lekin tu toh chalta hi jaa raha hai
Na le raha hai tu rukne ka naam
Aur is daud mein koshish hai ki kar sakein
Apne aap ko sambhaalne ka kaam

Lekin achaanak se ab lag raha hai aisa
Ki dheemi ho gayi hai teri raftaar
Aur hum sab kar rahe hain bas ab
Tere guzar jaane ka intezaar

Ae waqt, tu lag raha hai aaj bahut lamba
Kya mera sabr tujh par kaabu kar paayega
Ae waqt, mujhe bas yeh bata de
Kya tu jaldi se nikal jaayega?

Dooriyan

Hum the ek duje ke dil ke paas
The ek duje ki zindagi mein bahut hi khaas
Phir aaya ek daur jab nahi rakh sake hum apne
rishte ko theek
Aur faasle badh gaye kaafi hamare beech

Ho gaye hum juda
Shaayad tha yeh waqt ka takaza
Magar socha ek doosre ke baare mein bahut
Aur mehsoos ki ek doosre ki kami bahut zyada

Lekin ki nahi koshish humne
Kam karne ki yeh dooriyan
Na jaane kaise the hamare haalaat
Na jaane kya thi hamaari majbooriyan

Ab jaake lagta hai
Kaash us waqt apne rishte pe kuch mehnat kar li
hoti
Toh aaj jaake ek saath rehne ki hamaari kismat
hoti

Iraada

Yeh dil kehta hai kabhi-kabhi ki duniya-daari
chhod doon
Kuch aise hain log jinse apna muh mod lo

Lekin phir aata hai yeh khayaal
Ki sab chhodne se hoga kya fayda
Bahut gham hoga kuch logon ko
Isliye badal diya maine apna iraada

Zindagi haseen tabhi hogi
Agar banaane ki haseen hum mein khud hogi
chaah
Bas jud jaana hai un logon ke saath
Jo dikhaayenge mujhe meri taqdeer ki raah

Toh faisla karna hai mujhe
Ki jab dil chaahe sab chod doon
Bas zaroorat hai us ek ishaare ki
Jiske balboote pe is khayaal ko poori tarah se tod
doon

Unke Saath

Unke saath hoti thi bahut saari baatein
Batorte rehte the hum apne rishte ki saugaatein
Lafzon ki adla-badli mein
Nikal jaate the din aur raatein
Zaroorat nahi thi aur kisi ki zindagi mein
Poori karne ki apni saari muraadein

Phir ek din aisa bhi aaya
Jab hum bas chup ho gaye
Kyunki ab lagta tha khamoshi mein behtar ho
sakti thi dil ki saari baatein

Ab woh samajhne lage the hamari khamoshiyan
Aur phir khatam ho gayi bas
Hamaare beech ki saari pareshaaniyan

Waapsi

Aaj laga andar kuch hil sa gaya
Rooh ka ek bhoola tukda waapas mil sa gaya

Jo ek lagaayi thi pukar
Woh kisi ne sun hi li
Woh jo intezar tha mera
Woh aaj khatam ho hi gaya

Woh jo khud se milne ki chaahat thi
Jo ek akeli shaam mein huyi hararat si thi
Jisko paane ke liye uthte the sawaal kismat par
Aaj mil gaya un ka jawaab, bina daale laanat
apne par

Woh jo aaya meri zindagi mein
Jaga di usne ek chaah
Kyunki jaane anjaane mein
Usne dikha di mujhe meri zindagi ki raah

Ab chal padi hoon main us raaste par
Jisme aayenge kayi mod
Lekin ek baat ka hai khud par ab yakeen
Yeh raasta le jaayega mujhe meri najaat ki or

Ankahi

Yeh dil kehta hai
Woh kuch ankahi baatein aaj bol hi doon
Dil mein dabaaye huye woh jazbaat aaj khol hi
doon

Yeh dil kehta hai
Apne aap se kuch aur baatein aaj kar hi loon
Apne aap ko jeene ki salah aaj phir se de hi doon

Yeh dil kehta hai
Apni tamanna ko awaaz aaj de hi doon
Apni chaahaton ke samundar mein ek dubki laga
hi loon

Yeh dil kehta hai
Apni rooh ke andar aaj jhaank hi loon
Apne aap se ek mulaaqat aaj kar hi loon

Yeh dil kehta hai
Tum kar rahe ho aaj bahut saari baatein
Kyunki aaj waqt hai poori karne ki dil ki saari
chaahatein

Naya

Aaj ki raat kuch hone ko hai
Ek naye din ka intezzar hone ko hai

Ek nayi tamanna jaagne ko hai
Ek nayi manzil ka raasta khulne ko hai

Kuch naye saathi milne ko hain
Kuch bhoole logon ki yaad aane ko hai

Kuch naye jazbaat mahsoos karne ko hain
Kuch bhooli bisri yaadein yaad aane ko hain

Woh jo chale gaye the, woh vaapas aane ko hain
Woh jo kahin jaana chahte the, woh wahan jaane
ko hain

Aaj ki raat kuch hone ko hai
Ek naye din ki shuruaat hone ko hai

Saaya

Yeh pata chala mere upar uska hamesha hai
saaya
Jab raat ke andhere mein, mann mein uska
khayaal aaya

Woh hai dhoop mein chaon ki tarah
Barsaat mein jaise boondon ki leher
Woh hai deta mujhe dilaasa
Har ek din, har ek peher

Na jaane aaya kahan se woh
Na jaane rahega kitne talak
Kahin ojhal na ho jaaye woh
Jaise hi jhapkayoon mein apni palak

Jo bhi ho, ek baat ka hai mujhe yakeen
Uska saaya bana rahega har pal mujh par
Nazar ke saamne na ho toh kya hua, woh dil
mein hai mere
Toh bas is khayaal ke saath hai nahi ab kisi bhi
baat ka darr

9 789360 942526